Maths Revision Booklet
for CCEA GCSE 2-tier specification
M6

Conor McGurk

Contents

Revision Exercise 1A

(non-calculator)

You must **not** use a calculator for this paper. Total mark for this paper is 50.
Figures in brackets printed down the right-hand side of pages indicate the marks awarded to each question or part question.
You should have a ruler, compasses, set-square and protractor.

1. Write the fraction $\frac{36}{48}$ in its lowest terms.

Answer _____ [1]

   (a) Write 10% as:
     (i) a decimal,

Answer _____ [1]

     (ii) a fraction in its lowest terms.

Answer _____ [1]

   (b) Calculate:
     (i) ⅗ of 35

Answer _____ [2]

     (ii) 40% of 120

Answer _____ [2]

2. Complete the table below.

Shape	Order of rotational symmetry	Lines of symmetry
Rectangle		
Equilateral triangle		
Parallelogram		

[6]

3. Two angles of a parallelogram are in the ratio 3:2
    Find the size of the angles in the parallelogram.

        Answer _____°, _____°, _____°, _____° [4]

4.

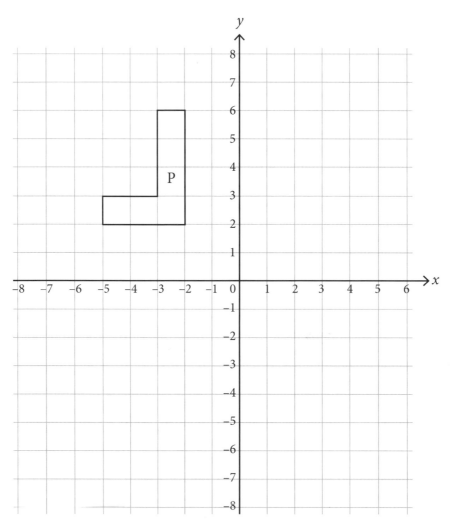

(a) Show the position of P after a translation:

   $\begin{pmatrix} 5 \\ -4 \end{pmatrix}$

   Label the new shape Q.

                                                                    [1]

(b) Reflect the shape P in the line $y = 1$
    Label this reflection R.

                                                                    [2]

5. A school holds a draw to raise funds.
   Each of the 600 pupils in the school buys a ticket in the draw.
   The tickets are numbered 1 to 600.

   (a) What is the probability that the ticket number 169 wins the draw?

   Answer _____ [1]

   (b) Find the probability that a ticket with a number greater than 400 wins the draw.

   Answer _____ [2]

   (c) One of the teachers says that the probability of a girl winning the draw is ½

   (i) Explain why this may not be true.

   Answer _____ [1]

   (ii) If the teacher is correct, how many girls attend the school?

   Answer _____ [1]

6. Find the solution set of the inequality

   $-15 \leq 5n < 20$

   and represent the solution on the number line below.

[4]

7. Letty drives her car to Coleraine.
   She drives at an average speed of 50 miles per hour for the first half hour.
   She then stops for petrol for 10 minutes.
   Letty drives the rest of the journey to Coleraine at an average speed of 60 miles per hour.
   The total time for her journey is 1 hour 15 minutes.

   (a) On the grid below, draw the distance/time graph for the total journey.   [3]

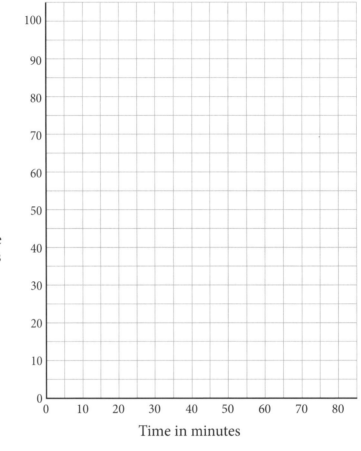

Distance in miles

Time in minutes

   (b) What is the average speed for the total journey?

                                                    Answer _____ miles per hour [2]

8. The nth term of a sequence is $3n - 1$
   The nth term of another sequence is $n^2 - 2$
   What are the 3 numbers between 1 and 30 which belong to both sequences?

                                              Answer _____, _____, _____ [3]

9. Roger records the scores of the Ulster rugby team in every game during the course of the season.
   The results are shown in the bar chart below.

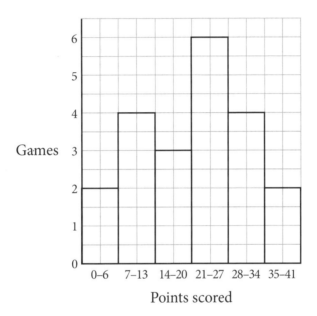

   The team are about to play the last match of the season.
   (a) Estimate the probability of the team scoring more than 20 points in the game.

                                                          Answer _____ [2]

   (b) Give 2 reasons why your estimate may not be very accurate.

       Answer _____ [1]

       Answer _____ [1]

10. Divide £108 in the ratio 3:1

Answer £_____ : £_____ [2]

11. A lorry driver uses the formula

C = 60M + 3T

to calculate costs for delivery, where M is the number of miles travelled and T is the time in hours to complete the delivery.
Change the subject of the formula to T.

Answer T = _____ [2]

12. There are a number of sweets in a bag.
The sweets have two flavours – toffee and peppermint.
There are 24 toffee sweets in the bag.
The probability of selecting a toffee sweet from the bag is ¼
How many peppermint sweets are in the bag?

Answer _____ sweets [2]

13. A is a point above the line BC.
Construct the perpendicular from the point A to the line BC.

A

B  C

[3]

Revision Exercise 1B

(non-calculator)

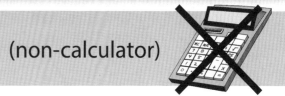

You must **not** use a calculator for this paper. Total mark for this paper is 50.
Figures in brackets printed down the right-hand side of pages indicate the marks awarded to each question or part question.
You should have a ruler, compasses, set-square and protractor.

1. A head teacher wishes to buy a selection box for each pupil in her school at Christmas.
    There are 173 pupils in the school.
    Selection boxes can be bought more cheaply in packs of 8.
    What is the least number of packs which the head teacher needs to buy?

    Answer _____ packs [2]

2. Here is a list of numbers.

    2, 3, 8, 16, 20, 24

    From the list select:

    (a) (i) a square number,

    Answer _____ [1]

    (ii) a cube number.

    Answer _____ [1]

    (b) Write down a number between 60 and 70 which is both a square number and a cube number.

    Answer _____ [1]

3. A fair 3-sided spinner is spun and a dice is tossed.

The **sum** of the two numbers is recorded in the table below.

		Dice					
		1	2	3	4	5	6
Spinner	1	2	3	4	5	6	7
	2	3	4				
	3	4	5	6			

(a) Complete the table to show the possible outcomes. [1]

(b) What is the probability that the outcome is a square number?

Answer _____ [2]

(c) What is the probability that the outcome is a prime number?

Answer _____ [2]

4. A, B and C are three ships.

B
✕

C
✕

A ✕

(a) Measure the bearing of B from A.

Answer _____° [1]

(b) What is the bearing of C from A?

Answer _____° [1]

5. Tickets for a concert are sold at £29.50 each.
    795 tickets are sold.
    The rental for the concert venue is £5995
    The rest of the sales money is given to the local hospital.
    Estimate the amount of money that the hospital receives.

                                        Answer _____ [3]

6. Sasha is going on a long journey.
    On day 1, she travels ⅓ of the journey.
    On day 2, Sasha travels ¼ of the journey.
    On the **final** 3rd day, she travels the **remaining** 125 miles.
    How long was the journey?

                                        Answer _____ miles [5]

7. Construct the bisector of the angle XYZ.

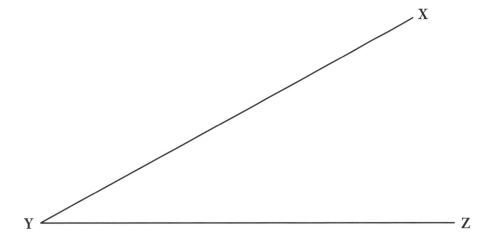

                                                            [3]

8. **(a)** Change the binary number 101111 into base 10 (decimal).

                                        Answer _____ [1]

    (b) Write the decimal number 41 in binary.

                                        Answer _____ [1]

9. **(a)** What is the next number in the following sequence?

1, 4, 9, 16, 25, 36, ………..

Answer _____ [1]

(b) Write down the nth term of the sequence

4, 9, 14, 19, …………….

Answer _____ [2]

10. The finishing scores of the top 200 golfers in the first round of a tournament were recorded.
The table shows the probability of the finishing score falling in each bracket.

Finishing score	Probability
60 – 64	0.05
65 – 69	0.15
70 – 74	0.45
75 – 79	0.25
80 or more	

(a) What is the probability that a golfer scored 80 or more?

Answer _____ [2]

(b) How many golfers had a score of 80 or more?

Answer _____ golfers [2]

11. Moya wishes to buy bathroom wall tiles. Each of the large tiles are in the shape of a regular octagon.
They are placed together as shown below.
Show that the tile in the centre between the octagonal tiles must be a square tile.

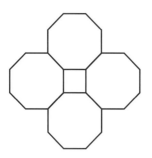

[4]

12. Find the values of the **integer** n where

$-15 \leq 3n < 8$

and represent the solutions on the number line below.

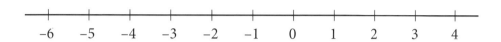

[4]

13. Two goats are tied in the opposite corners A and C of a field ABCD.
The field is 40 m long by 25 m wide and the goats are each tied with a rope which is 25 m long.
Using a scale of 1 cm = 5 m, draw a scale drawing of the field.
Show the area which each goat can graze and shade in the common area which both goats can graze.

A

C

[3]

14.

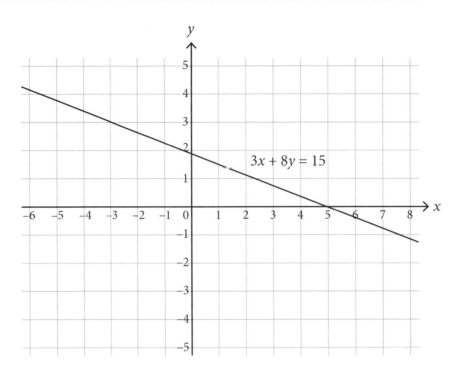

The line $3x + 8y = 15$ is drawn on the grid above.

By drawing the line $y = -x$ on the grid, find the solution to the pair of simultaneous equations

$3x + 8y = 15$ and $y = -x$

Answer $x = $ _____ , $y = $ _____ [2]

15. The table shows information about the drinks chosen by children at a party.

Drink	Orange	Cola	Milk	Water
Number	10	6	x	$3x + 4$

A child is chosen at random.

The probability of the child choosing orange is $\dfrac{1}{4}$.

Another child is chosen at random.

Find the probability that they choose water.

Answer _____ [5]

Revision Exercise 2A   (with calculator)

1. (a) If the length of a pencil is measured as 20 cm correct to the nearest centimetre, shade in the region on the number line which contains the pencil length.

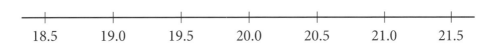

18.5	19.0	19.5	20.0	20.5	21.0	21.5

[2]

(b) If n is a whole number, what type of whole number is $2n - 1$?

Answer _____ [1]

(c) (i)   Write down the next number in the following sequence:

1, 3, 6, 10, ...

Answer _____ [1]

(ii)   What is the term to term rule in this sequence?

Answer _____ [1]

(iii)   What name is given to this special sequence of numbers?

Answer _____ [1]

2. Enlarge the shape below by a scale factor 2 from the centre A.

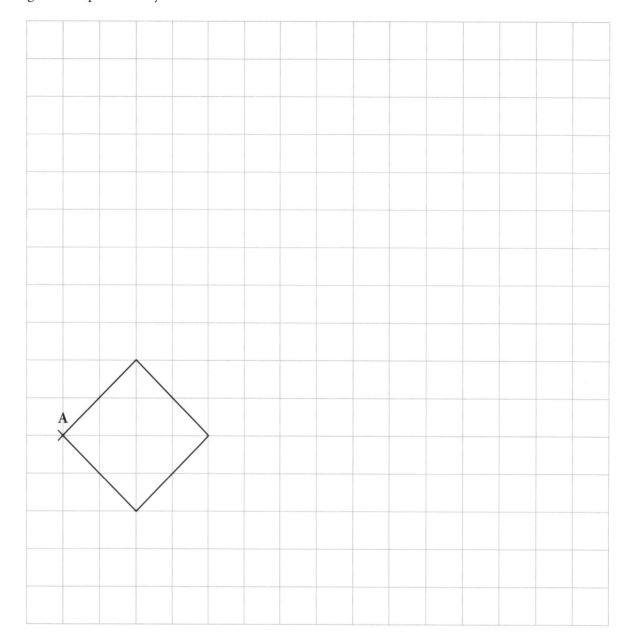

[2]

3. Bernadette buys a Christmas turkey.
    The turkey weighs 10 kg.
    Approximately what weight is the turkey in pounds (lb)?

    Answer _____ lb [2]

4. In a Maths class, the probability of selecting a student at random with brown hair is 0.4
    What is the probability of selecting a student who does not have brown hair?

    Answer _____ [2]

5. The map below shows landmarks in a town.
   The scale of the map is 1 cm = 500 m.

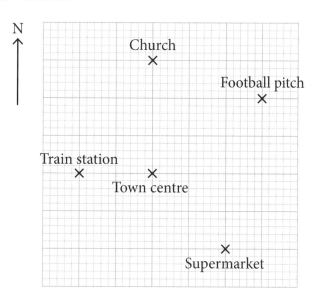

(a) What is due west of the town centre?

Answer _____ [1]

(b) What is south-east of the town centre?

Answer _____ [1]

(c) Find the bearing of the church from the train station.

Answer _____ ° [2]

(d) Using the scale above, calculate the distance from the train station from the football pitch.

Answer _____ m [3]

6. Sean is going to Los Angeles on holidays.
   He changes £900 into dollars.
   £1 sterling = $1.32

   (a) How many dollars does he receive?

   Answer $ _____ [2]

   (b) A bottle of perfume costs £49.99 in the airport in Belfast.
       In Los Angeles, the same bottle of perfume costs $63.50

       Is the Belfast or Los Angeles price the better value, and by how much?
       Give your answer in £ sterling.

   Answer _____ by £ _____ [3]

7. A bag contains 3 red balls, 4 blue balls and 5 green balls.
   What is the probability of choosing a blue ball at random from the bag?

   Answer _____ [2]

8. ABCD is a rhombus.
   Angle A is 42°

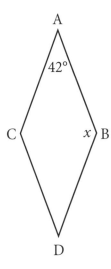

   Find the value of x in degrees.

   Answer _____ ° [3]

9. (a) Complete the table of values for $y = x^2 - x - 2$

x	−3	−2	−1	0	1	2	3
y	10			−2	−2	0	4

[3]

(b) On the grid below, draw the graph of $y = x^2 - x - 2$ for the values in the table above.

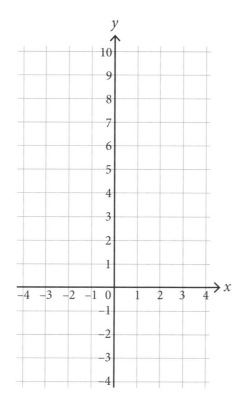

(c) Find the coordinates of the turning point of the graph.

Answer (_____ , _____) [2]

(d) Find the values of x where the line $y = ½$ crosses the graph.

Answer $x = $ _____ , _____ [2]

10. One of the solutions to the equation $x^3 + 4x = 29$ lies between 2 and 3
Use the method of **trial and improvement** to find this solution to one decimal place.

Answer $x = $ _____ [3]

11. The most popular colours of cars sold in the UK in 2018 were white, silver, black and blue.
A survey was carried to see which of the four colours was most popular in Belfast.
The four colours of one thousand cars were observed passing along the Westlink.
The probability of observing each colour is shown in the table below.

Colour	White	Silver	Black	Blue
Probability	0.34	0.27	0.22	

(a) What was the probability of observing a Blue car?

Answer _____ [2]

(b) What was the probability of observing a Silver or Black car?

Answer _____ [2]

(c) A second survey was carried out on the Westlink with five thousand cars being observed. The result for the most popular colour, white, was 0.36

Which of the surveys do you think is the most accurate? Give a reason for your answer.

Answer _____ survey since _____ [2]

12. The perimeter of a rectangle is 78 metres.
The ratio of the length to the breadth of the rectangle is 8:5
Find the area of the rectangle.

Answer _____ m² [4]

Revision Exercise 2B

(with calculator)

1. The instructions for cooking a turkey are as follows:

   Cooking time = 20 minutes per pound plus an extra 30 minutes.

   (a) How many minutes will it take to cook a 12 lb turkey?

   Answer _____ minutes [1]

   (b) If the turkey is placed in the oven at 2.00 pm, at what time will it be cooked?

   Answer _____ pm [1]

   (c) It takes 6 hours and 10 minutes to cook another turkey.
   From the cooking instructions above, work out the mass of the turkey in lb.

   Answer _____ lb [2]

2. The average contents of a box of matches is 72 matches.
   Mary buys 20 boxes and counts the number of matches in each box.
   The results are shown in the table below.

Number of matches	Fewer than 72	Exactly 72	More than 72
Number of boxes	4	14	2

   (a) Find the probability that one of the boxes selected at random contains fewer than 72 matches.

   Answer _____ [1]

   (b) A carton of match boxes contains 960 boxes.
   How many boxes would you expect to contain exactly 72 matches?

   Answer _____ boxes [3]

3. Two triangles, A and F, are shown on the grid below.

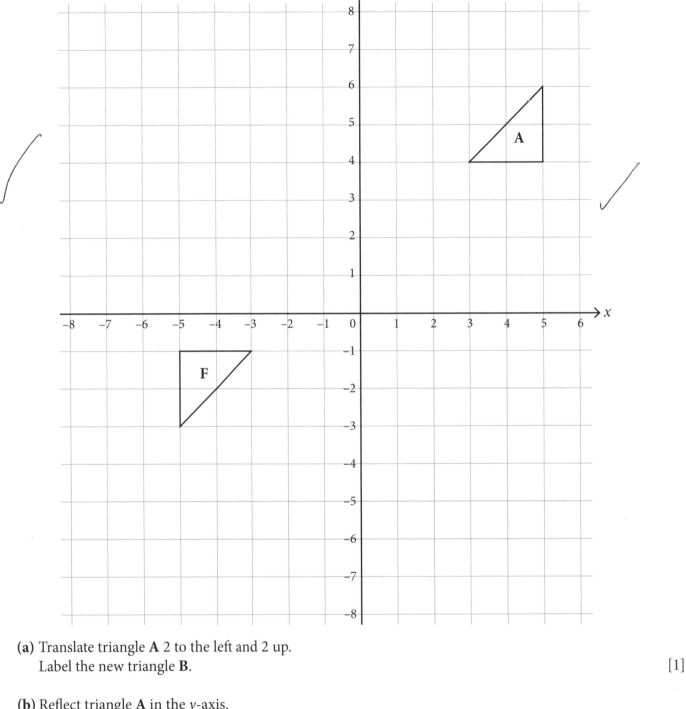

(a) Translate triangle **A** 2 to the left and 2 up.
Label the new triangle **B**. [1]

(b) Reflect triangle **A** in the *y*-axis.
Label this reflection **C**. [1]

(c) Reflect triangle **A** in the line *y* = 1
Label this reflection **D**. [2]

(d) Rotate triangle **D** 90° clockwise about the origin.
Label this image **E**. [3]

(e) Describe the transformation that maps triangle **E** onto triangle **F**.

Answer _____ [2]

4. A car manufacturer wishes to test the fuel consumption of a new car.
    The table below shows the number of miles travelled based on a full tank of 80 litres.

Litres remaining	80	65	30	10
Distance travelled (miles)	0	165	550	770

(a) On the grid below, plot the points and draw a straight line.   [3]

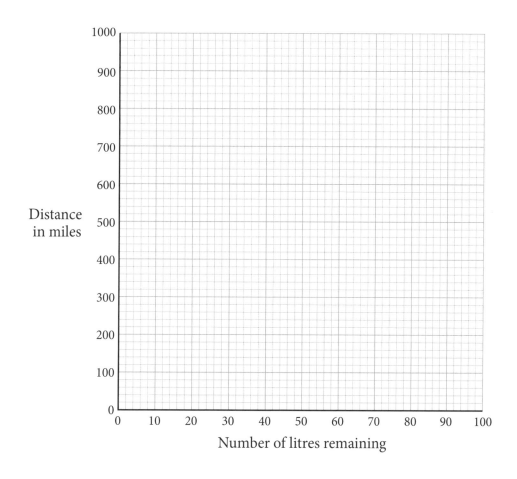

Distance in miles

Number of litres remaining

(b) Use your graph to estimate the total distance travelled on a full tank.

Answer _____ miles [1]

(c) How many litres are in the tank when the car has travelled 300 miles?

Answer _____ litres [1]

(d) What does the gradient of this graph represent in real life?

Answer _____ [1]

(e) Do you think the data in the table above is realistic? What might affect the number of litres used
    compared to the distance travelled by the car?

Answer _____ , because _____ [1]

5. Simplify:

(a) $x^3 \times x^5$

Answer _____ [1]

(b) $4x^6 \div 2x^2$

Answer _____ [1]

6. The shape below is a regular pentagon.

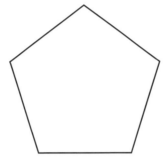

(a) Calculate the exterior angle of the regular pentagon.

Answer _____ ° [2]

(b) The shape below is a regular pentagon.

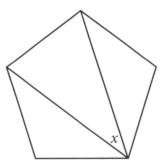

Calculate the size of the angle x.

Answer _____ ° [3]

7. The side of a cube is x cm.
    The volume of the cube is 100 cm³

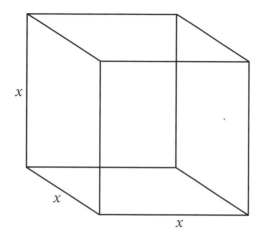

Use the method of trial and improvement to find the side of the cube to one decimal place.

Answer _____ [4]

8. Tickets are available for 4 areas of a sports ground:
   - the Covered Stand,
   - the Uncovered Stand,
   - the Town Terrace at one end of the ground, and
   - the Railway Terrace at the other end of the ground.

   The table below shows the probability of a spectator choosing where to watch a game in the sports ground on a particular Saturday.

Ticket	Covered Stand	Uncovered Stand	Town Terrace	Railway Terrace
Probability	0.36	0.27		0.18

   (a) Complete the table above.

   [2]

   (b) Both terraces are for standing only. Both stands are for seated spectators.
       If 11 500 spectators attend the match, how many were seated?

   Answer _____ spectators [3]

9. (a) The first 4 terms in a sequence are

       5   8   11   14

   Write down, in terms of n, an expression for the nth term of the sequence.

   Answer _____ [2]

   (b) Is the number 300 a term in this sequence?
       Give a reason for your answer.

   Answer _____ because _____ [2]

10. The formula

    $9C = 5F - 160$

    is used for converting temperature in degrees Fahrenheit (F) into degrees Celsius (C).
    Rearrange the formula to make F the subject.

    Answer $F = $ _____ [2]

11. Elaine, Georgina and Jackie spin the spinner below a number of times and record the results of the number of times a 1 is scored.

The table below shows the results of the spins.

	Number of spins	Number of 1s	Relative Frequency
Elaine	50	9	
Georgina	100	24	
Jackie	200	32	

(a) Complete the relative frequencies in the table above.

[3]

(b) Which girl's result gives a more reliable estimate of the likelihood of spinning a 1 on this spinner?
Give a reason for your answer.

Answer _____ because _____ [1]

12. One angle of a triangle is twice the size of the smallest angle in the triangle.
The third angle of the triangle is 3 times the size of the smallest angle.
Show that the triangle is a right angled triangle.

[3]

Problem Solving Questions

Note: *The new CCEA GCSE in Mathematics has an increased weighting for problem solving tasks: 25% AO3 for Foundation tier and 30% for Higher tier.*

A problem solving question is one where the student will, most likely, not see an immediate method for solving it. Hence, the student should persevere with the problem using a range of strategies. This section contains some problem solving questions to help students to practice working in this way. See CCEA's GCSE Mathematics microsite for further problem solving examples.

1. By placing + and – signs in the boxes below, make the equation correct.

    2 ☐ 3 ☐ 4 ☐ 5 ☐ 6 = 0

                                                                              [3]

2. **(a)** Write down two prime numbers which add up to 36.

                                                    Answer _____ [1]

    (b) Find another **three** pairs of prime numbers which also add up to 36.

          Answer _____ , _____ , _____ [3]

3. The shape shown below consists of four congruent (identical) right-angled triangles. Find the area of the shape.

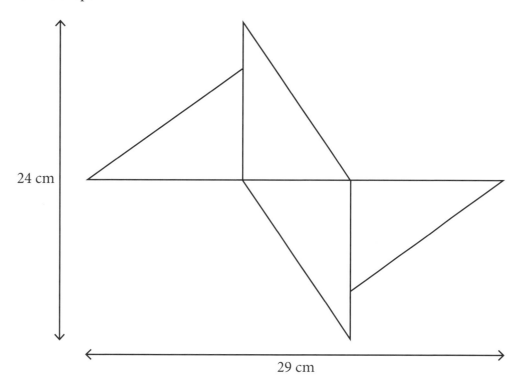

24 cm

29 cm

Answer _____ cm² [5]

Answers

Note: Marks are given in square brackets beside each question, broken down to indicate whether the marks are for the method [M], for the final answer [A] or for both the method and the final answer together [MA].

Revision Exercise 1A

1. **(a)** ¾ [A1] **(b) (i)** 0.1 [A1] **(ii)** $^{10}/_{100} = ^{1}/_{10}$ [A1]
   (c) (i) ⅕ of 35 = 7 so ⅗ = 21 [A1A1] **(ii)** 10% of 120 = 12 so 40% = 12 × 4 = 48 [A1A1]

2.

Shape	Order of rotational symmetry	Lines of symmetry
Rectangle	2	2
Equilateral triangle	3	3
Parallelogram	2	0

[A1] each correct answer.

3. A parallelogram has two pairs of equal angles which add up to 360° so $x + y = 180°$. [MA1] Ratio of 3:2 gives 5 shares so one share = 180° ÷ 5 = 36°. [MA1] 36 × 3 = 108 and 36 × 2 = 72 (i.e. 2 angles of 108° and 2 of 72°). MA2

4.

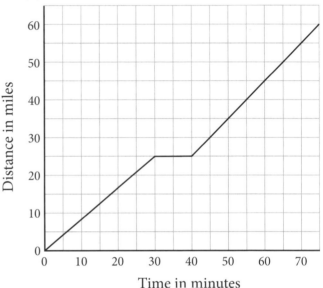

   (a) Q in correct position [A1] **(b)** R in correct position – line [A1] reflection [A1].

5. **(a)** ¹⁄₆₀₀ [MA1] **(b)** ²⁰⁰⁄₆₀₀ = ⅓ [M1A1]
   (c) (i) There may not be the same number of boys and girls in the school. [A1] **(ii)** Teacher being correct means probability = ½ so 300 girls. [A1]

6. $(-15 \leq 5n) \div 5$ [M1] giving $-3 \leq n$ so $n \geq -3$. [A1] $5n < 20 \div 5$ giving $n < 4$. [MA1] So we draw:

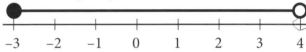

   The full circle indicates that −3 is included in the solution set but the empty circle at 4 indicates that 4 in not included in the solution. [A1]

7. **(a)**

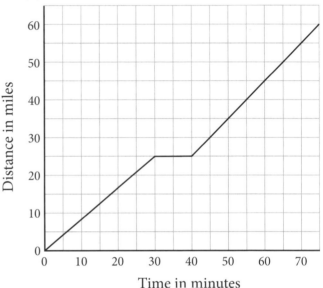

   [A3] for each line.
   (b) Covers 60 miles in 1 hour 15 minutes. 60 miles in 1¼ hours = 60 ÷ 1¼ = 48. [M1A1]

8. $3n - 1$ gives the terms $3(1) - 1, 3(2) - 1, \ldots$
   $= 2, 5, 8, 11, 14, 17, 20, 23, 26, 29, \ldots$ [MA1]
   $n^2 - 2$ gives the terms $(1)^2 - 2, (2)^2 - 2, (3)^2 - 2, \ldots$
   $= -1, 2, 7, 14, 23, 34, \ldots$ [MA1]
   The three terms are 2, 14 and 23. [A1]

9. **(a)** Probability of scoring more than 20 points = (number of games with score greater than 20 ÷ (total number of games)
   $= (6 + 4 + 2) \div (2 + 4 + 3 + 6 + 4 + 1)$
   $= 12 \div 21 = ^4/_7$ [M1A1]
   (b) Estimate of points scored takes no consideration of the opposition. Estimate of points scored takes no consideration of your team's injuries or the strength of your team. Estimate of points scored takes no consideration of weather conditions etc. [MA1] for each correct suggestion.

10. $108 \div 4 = 27$ [MA1] $3 \times 27 = 81$ so £81:£27 [MA1]
11. $C - 60M = 3T$ [MA1]; $T = (C - 60M) \div 3$ [MA1]
12. Probability of toffee sweet = ¼ which represents 24 sweets. Therefore, ¾ of the sweets are peppermint = $24 \times 3 = 72$ peppermint sweets. [M1A1]
13. Take the compasses and open it out so that the distance is a little longer that the distance of A from the line BC. Place the point of the compasses at A and draw two arcs cutting the line BC to the left and right of the point A. Label the points D and E. [MA1] Place the point of the compasses at D and draw an arc below the line BC. Using the same compasses width, place the point of the compasses at E and draw an arc below the line BC to intersect with the arc drawn from D. Where these arcs intersect, label this point F. [MA1] Use a ruler to join A and F. This line AF is the perpendicular from A to BC. [A1]

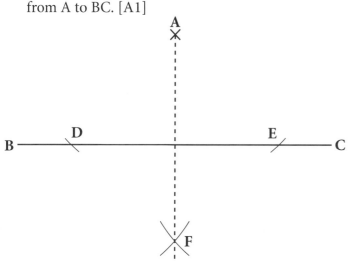

Revision Exercise 1B

1. $173 \div 8 = 21.62\ldots$ [MA1] 22 packs. [A1]
2. (a) (i) 16 [MA1] (ii) 3⁴ [MA1] (b) 64 [MA1]
3. (a) Missing entries First row: 5, 6, 7, 8. Second row: 7, 8, 9. [MA1] (b) 4/18 (= 2/9) [M1A1]
   (c) 9/18 (= ½) [M1A1]
4. (a) Bearing of 043° (need zero in front of 4). [A1]
   (b) Bearing 152°. [A1]
5. 800 tickets at £30 each = £24,000 [M1A1]
   £24,000 minus £6,000 rental = £18,000 [MA1]
6. $\frac{1}{3} + \frac{1}{4} = \frac{4}{12} + \frac{3}{12} = \frac{7}{12}$. [M1A1] On the 3rd day she travels $1 - \frac{7}{12} = \frac{5}{12}$. [MA1] $\frac{5}{12} = 125$ miles so $\frac{1}{12} = 125 \div 5 = 25$ miles. [MA1] So total journey = $25 \times 12 = 300$. [MA1]
7. Place the point of the compasses at the point Y and using the same compasses width, mark arcs on the lines XY and ZY. [MA1] Next place the point of the compasses on the arc on XY and draw an arc between the lines XY and ZY. Repeat for the arc on

ZY so that the arcs drawn cut each other. [MA1] Finally, join the intersection of the arcs to the point Y. This dotted line bisects (cuts in half) the angle XYZ. [MA1]

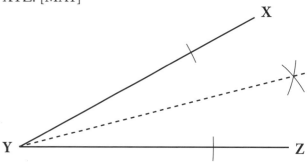

8. (a) 32 16 8 4 2 1
      1 0 1 1 1 1 = $32 + 8 + 4 + 2 + 1$
      = 47 in base 10 [MA1]
   (b) $41 = 32 + 8 + 1$, so: 32 16 8 4 2 1
                               1 0 1 0 0 1 [MA1]
9. (a) 49. (b) Difference between the terms is 5. Hence, the 1st term begins $5n$. 1st term is $4 = 5(1) - 1$. So nth term is $5n - 1$.
10. (a) Probability of 80 or more
       = $1 - (0.05 + 0.15 + 0.45 + 0.25) = 0.10$ [M1A1]
    (b) Number of golfers scoring 80 or more
       = $0.1 \times 200 = 20$ [M1A1]
11. 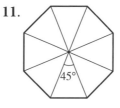 8 equal sides means 8 equal angles at centre = $360 \div 8 = 45°$. [MA1] So the interior angle of a octagon is 135°. [MA1] Angles at corner of the central tile are two octagon internal angles = $135° + 135°$ = 270°. Hence the third angle is 360° minus 270° = 90° [MA1]. So the central tile must be a square as all sides equal and all angles are 90°. [MA1]
12. $-15 \leq 3n \div 3$ [M1] giving $-5 \leq n$ so $n \geq -5$. [MA1] $3n < 8 \div 3$ giving $n < 2.66\ldots$ [MA1]. So we draw:

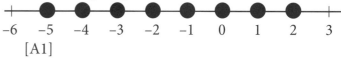
[A1]
13. Rectangle ABCD [M1A1]. With compasses at A, radius 5 cm, draw a large arc to cut sides AB and CD. Repeat for compasses at C: draw a large arc to cut sides AB and CD [MA1]. Shade solution area for [MA1]. (See sketch below.)

14.

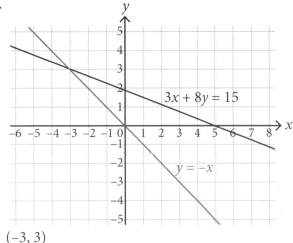

$3x + 8y = 15$

$y = -x$

(−3, 3)

15. Probability of choosing orange = ¼ = 10 children. So there are 10 × 4 = 40 children at the party [MA1]. Hence 10 + 6 + x + 3x + 4 = 40 [MA1], so 4x + 20 = 40 giving x = 5 [MA1]. Hence 3x + 4 = 3(5) + 4 = 19 [MA1]. Probability of choosing water = ¹⁹⁄₄₀ [MA1].

Revision Exercise 2A

1. (a) Between 19.5 and 20.5. [A2] (b) Odd number [A1] (c) (i) 15 [A1] (ii) Add 2, add 3, add 4 (increase by one each time). [A1] (iii) Triangular numbers [A1]

2.

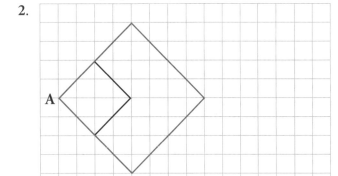

A

[MA2]

3. 1 kg = 2.2 lb (this fact needs to be known) [A1]
    10 kg = 2.2 × 10 = 22 lb [MA1]

4. 1 − 0.4 = 0.6 [M1A1]

5. (a) Train station [A1] (b) Supermarket [A1] (c) 034 ([A1] for angle [A1] for including the zero.)
    (d) 5.4 cm = 500 × 5.4 = 2700 [A1M1A1]

6. (a) 900 × 1.32 = $1188 [M1A1]
    (b) 63.50 ÷ 1.32 = £48.11 [M1A1]
    Los Angeles by £49.99 − £48.11 = £1.88 [MA1]

7. ⁴⁄₁₂ (= ⅓) [M1A1]

8. ABCD is a rhombus, opposite angles are equal. Hence, angle C is 42° [MA1]. Thus, sum of angles B and D equal 360° − 42° − 42° = 276° [MA1]. So x = 276° ÷ 2 = 138° [MA1].

9. (a)

x	−3	−2	−1	0	1	2	3
y	10	4	0	−2	−2	0	4

[A2]

(b)

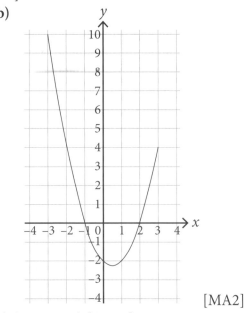

[MA2]

(c) (0.5, −2.25) [A1A1]
(d) x = 2.2 approx and −1.2 approx [A1A1].

10. x = 2: 2^3 + 4(2) = 16
    x = 3: 3^3 + 4(3) = 39
    x = 2.5: $(2.5)^3$ + 4(2.5) = 25.625
    x = 2.6: $(2.6)^3$ + 4(2.6) = 27.976
    x = 2.7: $(2.7)^3$ + 4(2.7) = 30.483 [MA1]
    x = 2.65: $(2.65)^3$ + 4(2.65) = 18.609625 + 10.6
    = 29.209625 [MA1]
    So x = 2.6 to 1 decimal place [MA1]

11. (a) 1 − (0.34 + 0.27 + 0.22) = 0.17 [M1A1]
    (b) Silver or black = 0.27 + 0.22 = 0.49 [M1A1]
    (c) The second survey was more accurate as they observed 5000 cars and the first survey observed 1000 cars. The greater number in the experiment provides a more accurate result. [MA2]

12. Perimeter = 2 × (length + breadth) = 78
    length + breadth = 78 ÷ 2 = 39 [MA1]. Divide 39 in the ratio 8:5 i.e. 13 shares: 39 ÷ 13 = 3, so:
    length = 3 × 8 = 24; breadth = 3 × 5 = 15 [M1A1]
    Area = 15 × 24 = 360 m² [MA1]

Revision Exercise 2B

1. (a) 20 × 12 + 30 = 270 [MA1] (b) 270 ÷ 60
    = 4 hours and 30 minutes [A1] (c) 6 hours
    10 minutes = 6 × 60 + 10 = 370 minutes [MA1].
    Subtract extra 30 minutes gives 370 − 30 = 340.
    340 ÷ 20 minutes per lb = 17 lb [MA1].

2. (a) ⁴⁄₂₀ (= ⅕) [MA1]
    (b) Probability of exactly 72 = ¹⁴⁄₂₀ [MA1].
    Expected number = ¹⁴⁄₂₀ × 960 = 672 [M1A1]

3. **(a)** B has coords (1, 5), (3, 5) and (3, 7) [A1]
   (b) C has coords (–3, 3), (–5, 3) and (–5, 5) [A1]
   (c) D has coords (3, –1), (5, –1) and (5, –3) [A1A1]
   (d) E has coords (–1, –3), (–1, –5) and (–3, –5)
   [A1A1A1]
   (e) Reflection in the line $y = x$ [A1A1]

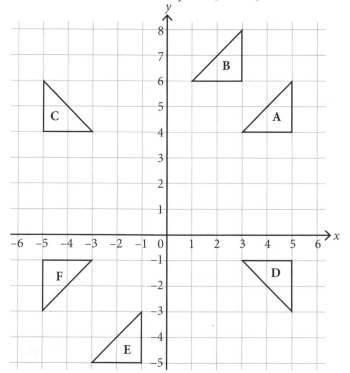

4. **(a)** Plotted (0, 80), (65, 165), (30, 550), (10, 770) [A2] and a straight line drawn [A1]. **(b)** Intercept on vertical axis 880 [MA1]. **(c)** Graph reading; approximately 52 [MA1]. **(d)** Miles per litre [MA1]. **(e)** No, because faster driving uses more fuel. Also motorway driving compared to city driving, bad roads and hold ups affect fuel consumption so litres used is not a linear process. ([A1] for any correct observation.)

5. **(a)** x^8 [MA1] **(b)** $2x^4$ [MA1]

6. **(a)** Regular pentagon 5 sides; so $360° ÷ 5 = 72°$ is the exterior angle [M1A1]. **(b)** Interior angle of pentagon $= 180° – 72° = 108°$ [MA1].

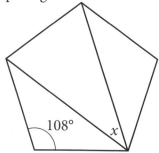

   Angles in isosceles triangles $= 180° – 108°$ $= 72° ÷ 2 = 36°$ [MA1]. Hence $x + 36 + 36 = 108$, giving $x = 36°$ [A1]

7. $x = 4$: $4^3 = 64$
   $x = 5$: $5^3 = 125$ [MA1]

$x = 4.5$: $(4.5)^3 = 91.125$
$x = 4.6$: $(4.6)^3 = 97.336$
$x = 4.7$: $(4.7)^3 = 103.823$ [MA1]
$x = 4.65$: $(4.65)^3 = 100.544625$ [MA1]
So $x = 4.6$ to 1 decimal place [MA1].

8. **(a)** $0.36 + 0.27 + 0.18 = 0.81$ [MA1]
   $1 – 0.81 = 0.19$ [MA1] **(b)** Probability of a spectator being seated $= 0.36 + 0.27 = 0.63$ [MA1]. Number of seated spectators $= 0.63 × 11500 = 7245$ [M1A1]

9. **(a)** $3n + 2$ [M1A1] **(b)** No. For a value of n, $3n + 2$ is a term in the sequence. So assuming $3n + 2 = 300$ [MA1], $3n = 298$ giving $n = 99⅓$ which is not possible. [MA1]

10. $9C = 5F – 160$; so $5F = 9C + 160$ [MA1].
    $F = (9C + 160) ÷ 5$ [MA1].

11. **(a)** Values from top to bottom: 0.18 (or correct fraction ¹⁸⁄₁₀₀ or ⁹⁄₅₀) [A1]; 0.24 [A1]; 0.16 [A1].
    (b) Jackie as there are a greater number of spins. [MA1]

12. Ratio of sides of triangle is 1:2:3 [MA1].
    Hence $180° ÷ (1 + 2 + 3) = 180° ÷ 6 = 30°$ [MA1].
    Three angles are 30°, 60° and 90° so triangle is right-angled (90°) [MA1].

Problem Solving Questions

1. The total of the numbers is $2 + 3 + 4 + 5 + 6 = 20$ [MA1]; Hence, in order for the solution to be zero, we need to add 10 and subtract 10 [M1];
   $10 = 2 + 3 + 5$ or $10 = 4 + 6$;
   so answer is $2 + 3 – 4 + 5 – 6 = 0$ [MA1]

2. **(a) (b)** Four pairs of prime numbers are:
   $5 + 31 = 36$ $7 + 29 = 36$
   $13 + 23 = 36$ $17 + 19 = 36$ [A1 each]

3. Label the vertices:

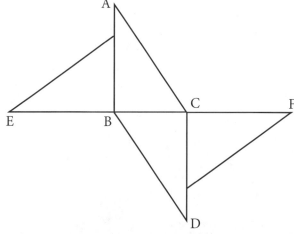

   AB = CD and AB + CD = 24 cm so AB = 12 [MA1]
   EB = CF and EB + CF = 24 cm so BC = 29 – 24 = 5 [MA1]. Area of triangle ABC $= ½BC × AB = ½ × 5 × 12 = 30$ [M1A1]; so area of 4 triangles $= 30 × 4 = 120$ cm² [MA1]

Updated to meet the requirements of the revised (2017 onwards) two-tier CCEA GCSE Mathematics specification, this is one of eight revision booklets to cover levels M1 to M8. These valuable questions were specially commissioned for the booklet and are not from past papers. Full answers are included at the rear and contain not only the final answer but, where appropriate, an indication of the process required to reach the given solution. The book has been through a meticulous quality assurance process by a GCSE Mathematics expert.

Which revision booklets do I need?

Students sitting CCEA GCSE Mathematics will be in one of four pathways and will require two revision booklets. The student's teacher will be able to advise which pathway they are studying.

If the student is studying this pathway...	...they will need these revision booklets
Foundation Tier Option 1	M1 and M5
Foundation Tier Option 2	M2 and M6
Higher Tier Option 1	M3 and M7
Higher Tier Option 2	M4 and M8

COLOURPOINT
EDUCATIONAL

£3.**99**

ISBN 978-1-78073-197-1

9 781780 731971

www.colourpoint.co.uk